KNOWLEDGE ENCYCLOPEDIA
LIVING THINGS

© Wonder House Books 2022

All rights reserved. No part of this book may be reproduced or transmitted in any form by any means, electronic or mechanical, including photocopying and recording, or by any information storage and retrieval system except as may be expressly permitted in writing by the publisher.

(An imprint of Prakash Books)

contact@wonderhousebooks.com

Disclaimer: The information contained in this encyclopedia has been collated with inputs from subject experts. All information contained herein is true to the best of the Publisher's knowledge. Maps are only indicative in nature.

ISBN : 9789354401848

Table of Contents

Life and Evolution	3
Our Diverse World	4–5
The Goldilocks Planet	6–7
Classifying Living Things	8–9
Bacteria and Archaea	10
Fungi	11
Inside a Plant	12–13
Algae, Bryophytes, and Pteridophytes	14
Gymnosperms	15
Angiosperms	16–17
Inside an Invertebrate	18–19
Parazoa and Radiata	20
Helminths and Annelids	21
Protostome Coelomates	22
Deuterostome Coelomates	23
Inside a Vertebrate	24–25
Poikilotherms	26–27
Homoiotherms	28–29
Habitats	30–31
Word Check	32

LIFE AND EVOLUTION

Living things are all the organisms that are, or once were, alive. From the wondrous microscopic bacteria to the great blue whales gliding in our oceans, from the terrifying dinosaurs who roamed our planet millions of years ago to the beautiful butterflies that flit in our gardens, all of this life came to be by a wonderful process called **evolution**. First suggested by Charles Darwin and Alfred Russell Wallace, this idea says that all creatures try to make more of themselves (reproduction) and try to fit as well as possible into their environment (adaptation). Some succeed more than others and leave behind more animals and plants of their kind. Others fail and go extinct. But when the climate changes or food becomes scarce or a new predator evolves, those who can change themselves survive. Those who cannot, like the dinosaurs, become extinct. This is called **natural selection**. In this book, we will explore the wonderful world of microbes, plants, and animals.

▼ *Fish swimming around a coral reef. They are both living things*

Our Diverse World

Our planet is divided into many climatic zones. Each of these zones has its own weather. The microbes, plants, and animals that grow in these zones are adapted to it. The plants and animals that naturally occur in large numbers in any **habitat** are called biomes. Many of the living beings in them are **endemic**, which means that they cannot live anywhere else. But many other beings can regularly come and go between these zones. These are called migratory.

🔍 Polar Zone

This is the icy world of polar bears (in the Arctic) and penguins (in Antarctica), but almost no plants grow here. This snowy world, called **tundra**, receives very little sunlight and remains in the dark for six months of the year.

◀ The white, furry coat of polar bears helps them retain heat and also acts as a camouflage

🔍 Subpolar Zone

The **taiga** region lies in Canada and Russia, full of great pine trees, grizzly bears, and white wolves. In the Southern Hemisphere, it is made of the Southern Ocean, where the humpback whales roam.

◀ Humpback whales hunt in groups by making 'nets' of bubbles in which they trap small fish

🔍 Temperate Zone

The temperate zone lies across Europe, China, North America and the southern tip of Argentina. It has long winters and short summers and is home to many animals and plants. Parts of it are forested, while the others make giant grasslands called the prairies in America, and steppes in Russia.

▲ Wheat, which grows mostly in the temperate zone, is the staple food of nearly a billion people

🔍 Mediterranean Zone

The Mediterranean zone is a small climatic zone found around the Mediterranean Sea, as well as parts of Australia, and California.

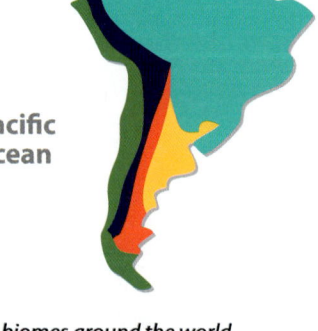
▲ Major biomes around the world

⭐ Incredible Individuals

Starting in 1954, the famous TV presenter David Attenborough recorded many programmes about the incredible diversity of life, helping promote awareness of ecological science and environmental conservation.

SCIENCE | LIVING THINGS

In Real Life

The Mariana Trench is Earth's deepest point. At 11,034 meters, it is too deep and dark to support much life. However, data suggests that microbial life does exist. Its deepest point is called the Challenger Deep, only four people have ever been to this frigid depth.

◀ Volcanoes on the seafloor provide heat and nutrients for microbes to thrive

▲ Camels store food and water in their humps to adapt to long journeys in the desert

🔍 Desert Zone

Deserts are found in all continents, often far from the sea, where there is little rain. Few plants grow in the desert, but they are adapted to the scarcity of water.

🔍 Mountain Zone

The mountain biome is found on the tall mountains, like the Himalayas and Andes. The animals and plants here have adapted to thin air and cold weather.

🔍 Tropical Zone

The tropical zone is the richest in the world in terms of plants, animals and microbes. The **rainforests** of the Amazon, Central Africa, and the Malay Archipelago lie within the tropical zone. It also includes the grasslands called **savanna**.

▲ The tropical rainforests have the largest share of Earth's biodiversity

🔍 The Ocean

The ocean has many **pelagic** biomes of its own, depending on how deep the water is. The deeper you go, the less oxygen there is, and the more the pressure of the seawater above you.

Most marine beings live within a depth of 200 metres in the **epipelagic zone**. This includes all the major fish species that human beings eat. It is made of estuaries, where rivers meet the sea, coral reefs that host hundreds of marine species and the open ocean. The **mesopelagic zone** has many kinds of sharks and jellyfish. As you go into the **bathypelagic zone**, sunlight begins to fade. Then in the **abyssopelagic zone**, it is completely dark. Marine animals that live here make their own light, like the angler fish.

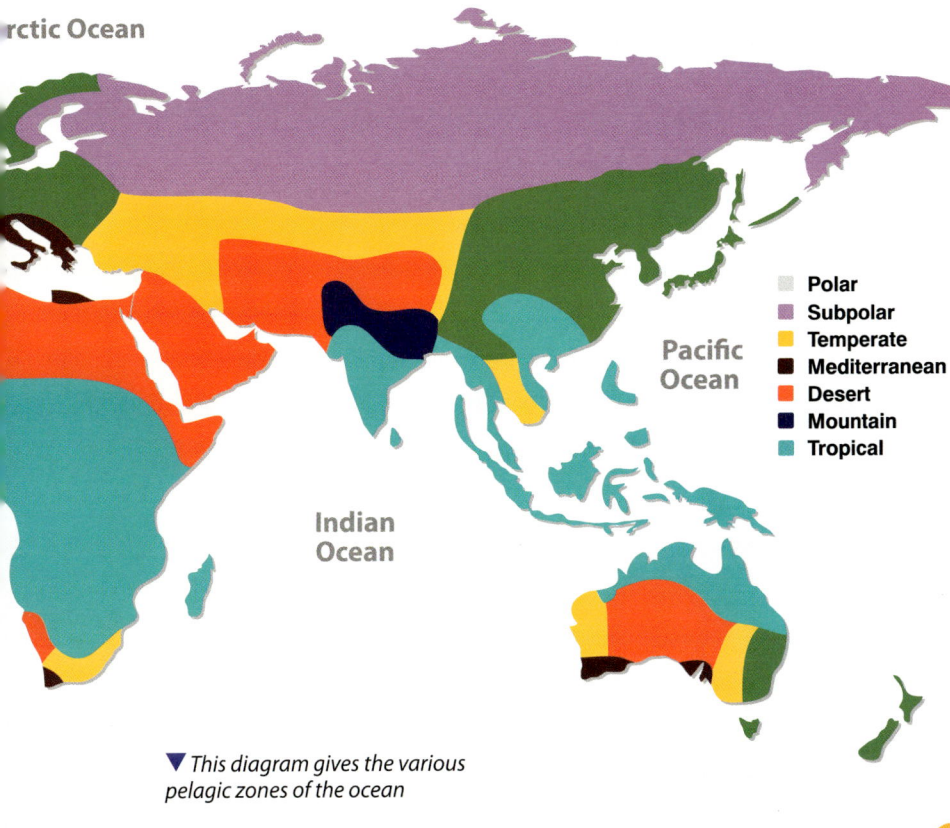

▼ This diagram gives the various pelagic zones of the ocean

The Goldilocks Planet

▼ The atmosphere traps enough heat from the Sun for life to prosper; no less and no more

Our planet Earth has been called the Goldilocks planet. It is 'just right' for life to flourish. It is neither too close to the Sun to be too hot, nor too far from it to be too cold. It has enough gravity so that the atmosphere that encircles Earth does not blow away.

Atmosphere

Our planet's atmosphere traps enough heat from the Sun so that the water on Earth is mostly in liquid state. A little hotter and most of the water would be vapour; a little colder and it would be ice. Liquid water creates the oceans where **marine beings** first evolved.

The atmosphere also has enough oxygen in it to allow terrestrial beings (beings that live on land and breathe air) to evolve. Radioactivity from within the Earth keeps its interiors liquid, which allows for volcanism, which brings fresh minerals to the surface. No other planet in our solar system has all these together.

Habitable Zone

Can there be life on other planets that revolve around a star far away from us? After studying the Earth, scientists have come up with the idea of the **habitable zone**, which has the right temperature, the right amount of light, and other conditions for life to thrive on any planet that is within it.

The habitable zone of our Sun is between 0.9–1.5 times the distance from the Earth to the Sun. But does such a planet exist elsewhere? In 2014, astronomers discovered Kepler-186f, an Earth-sized planet that revolves around a star 500 light years away from us, which is in the habitable zone of its sun.

▼ The habitable zone of a solar system depends on the size of its star

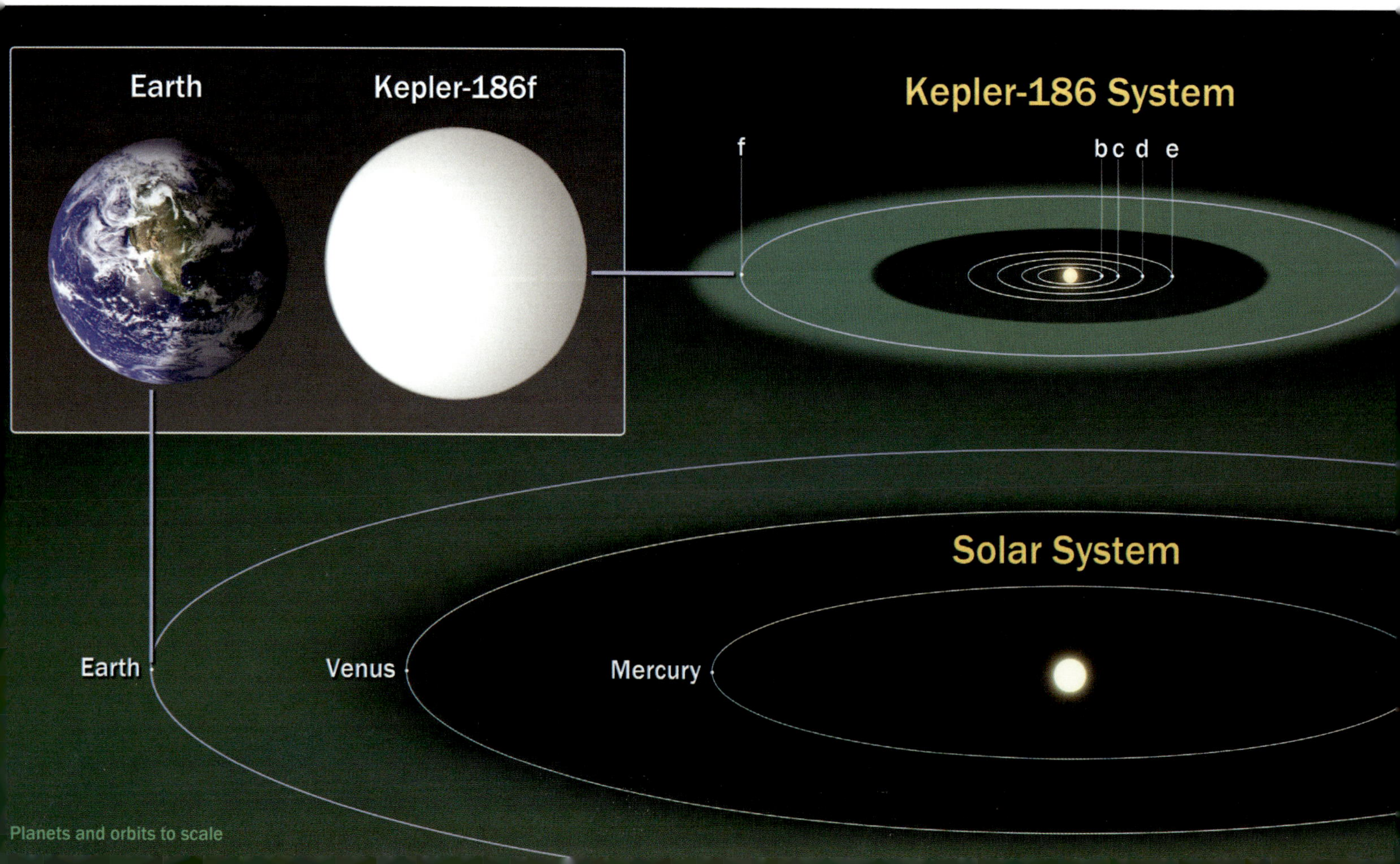

Planets and orbits to scale

SCIENCE | LIVING THINGS

⭐ Incredible Individuals

Charles Darwin was the first (with Alfred Russell Wallace) to suggest the Theory of Evolution. He began his career as a naturalist on board the British ship *HMS Beagle*, which sailed around the world collecting specimens of animals and plants. One of these visits was to the Galapagos Islands in the Pacific Ocean, where Darwin saw many different kinds of finches, which looked the same but had different kinds of beaks. This set him thinking, and he finally wrote his thoughts in a book that changed the world: *The Origin of Species*.

▲ Darwin began his research at the age of 22, but published it only after 28 years in 1859

🔍 The Moon

The Moon is in the habitable zone. So why does it not have life? That is because the Moon is **tidally locked** to Earth, so that one side is always facing us. This makes the temperatures extreme on the dark and light sides of the Moon. Also, the Moon's gravity is too weak to tie down its atmosphere. The Moon's atmosphere is extremely thin, containing gases like sodium and potassium which are absent from the Earth's atmosphere.

▶ There is a misconception that wolves howl at the Moon. That is untrue. Wolves howl at each other. The Moon just happens to be there!

🔍 Urey-Miller Experiment

Scientists think that life may have started on Earth not when it had plenty of oxygen, but when its atmosphere was comprised of gases like methane, ammonia, and hydrogen. The scientists Harold Urey and Stanley Miller tried an experiment, mixing these gases with water and running electricity through them. A week later, Miller and Urey found amino acids in the mix, the building blocks of life.

👤 In Real Life

The Movile Cave in Romania is pitch dark. It has an atmosphere made of poisonous gases, and has been cut off from the rest of the world for millions of years. Yet many unique species of animals live in it, feeding on the bacteria that make food from the poisonous gases. Scientists think it may be how life might evolve on other planets.

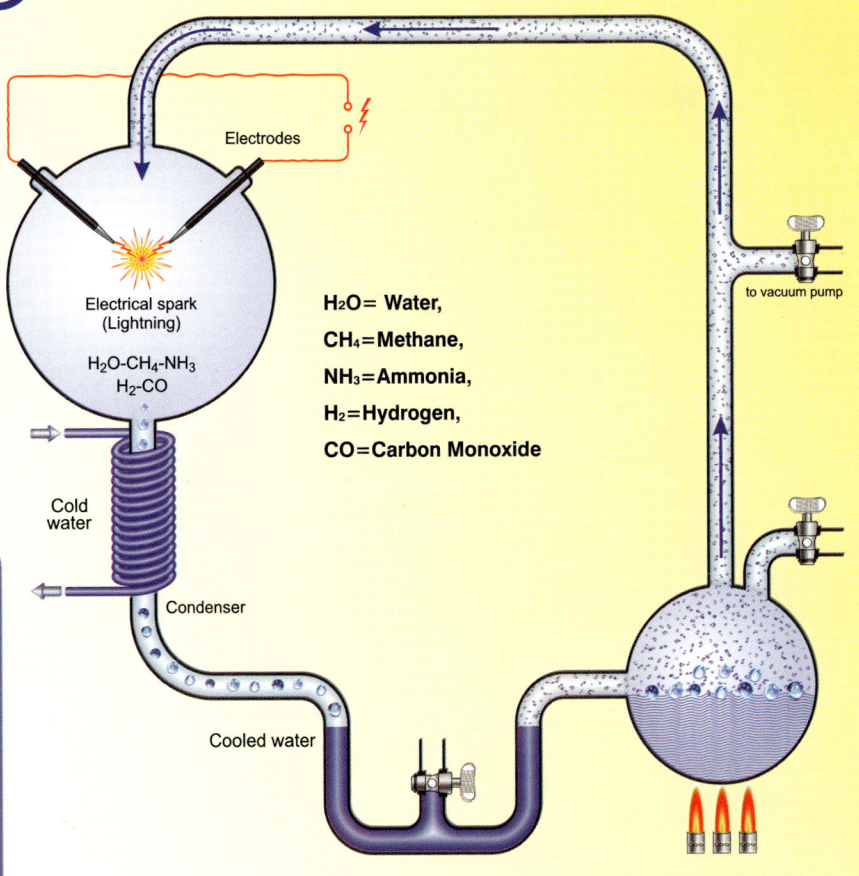

H_2O = Water,
CH_4 = Methane,
NH_3 = Ammonia,
H_2 = Hydrogen,
CO = Carbon Monoxide

▲ A diagram of the Urey-Miller experiment

Classifying Living Things

Two discoveries revolutionised the way scientists look at the living world. The first discovery, made in 1859, was called the Theory of Evolution. The second discovery, made in the early 20th century, claimed that all living things on our planet have the same **genetic code**. That meant that all life on this planet descended from a single ancestor, who may have lived over 3.5 billion years ago (or earlier).

Early Classification

Earlier, scientists would classify living organisms based on how similar they look to each other (for example, lions, tigers and cats all belong to one family). Now they use the study of DNA taken from these organisms. The science of classifying life is called taxonomy.

The Three Domains

DNA is present in all life forms and carries the recipe for making that being. Minor changes in the sequence of the DNA can lead to major differences in how the living being turns out, and that is how life evolves. This system of taxonomy divides all beings into three domains—Bacteria, Archaea, and Eukaryota. The last one includes all the **multicellular organisms** of the planet, including animals, fungi, and plants.

▲ Before DNA, biologists used the appearance of living beings to classify them

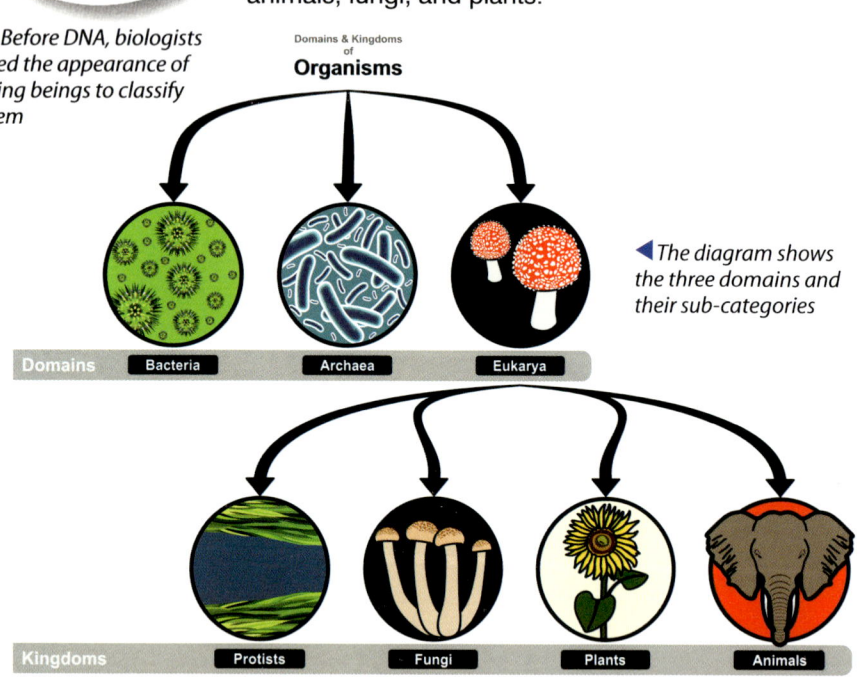

◀ The diagram shows the three domains and their sub-categories

Hierarchical Taxa

A **taxon** is a unit of classification (plural: taxa). Different taxa are arranged in ranks to form a hierarchy.

Domain: It is the highest level of classification. There are only three domains, in which humans are eukaryotes of the Eukarya domain.

Kingdom: It is the division of a domain. Until 1990, these were the highest level of classification. Unicellular prokaryotes were thought to make one kingdom, called Protista, but now scientists have found that the differences are too vast, so many taxa have their own kingdoms.

SCIENCE — LIVING THINGS

▲ Despite their differences, all dogs belong to the same species, *Canis lupus*

Phylum: This is the basic division of a kingdom. Some phyla (plural) may be bunched together to form sub-kingdoms. Earlier, **zoologists** divided them into vertebrates and invertebrates depending on whether they had a backbone or not. This is no more considered scientific, but it is still a useful classification.

Class: This is the division of a phylum, for example, the class Insecta or class Mammalia. Animals within a class share many similarities.

Order: Classes are divided into orders, which club animals that are similar. For example, the order Primates includes all animals that can climb trees, have colour vision and grasping hands, like monkeys, lemurs and apes.

▲ All cats belong to the family Felidae

Family: This is a group of really similar animals within a class, like cats (Felidae) or big apes (Hominidae).

Genus: Usually, all animals grouped in a genus look quite similar to each other, except for really minor differences. For example, lions and tigers are both grouped within the genus *Panthera*. Often, they can breed with each other. The genus and species name of an animal make up a living being's scientific name.

Species: This is the final unit. All the animals in a species should be able to breed with each other. For all of our differences, we human beings form one species in one genus—*Homo sapiens*.

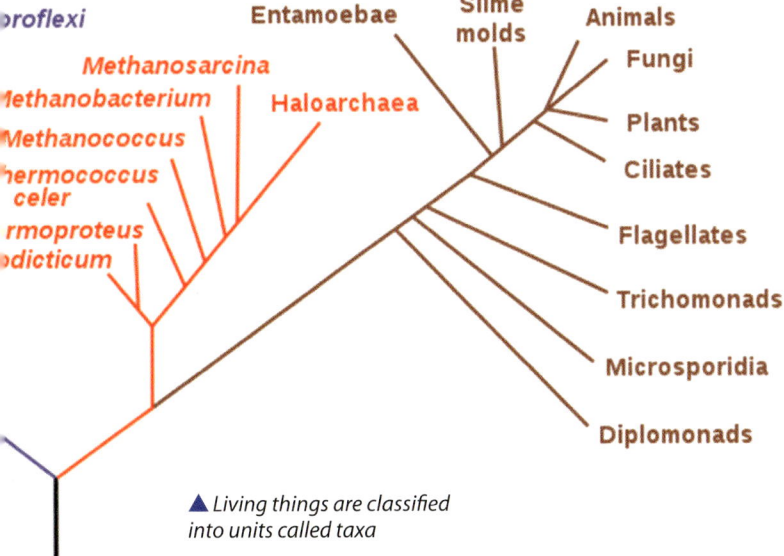

▲ Living things are classified into units called taxa

▶ All human beings, no matter their ancestry, belong to one species: *Homo sapiens*

Bacteria and Archaea

Bacteria and Archaea make up two of the three domains of the world, but they are quite simple to understand. They are both single-celled beings, made of a hard **cell wall**, a softer **cell membrane**, and a liquid matrix filled with proteins (cytoplasm) inside it. The **cytoplasm** is made of lots of enzymes that carry out many chemical reactions that keep them alive. The DNA of Bacteria and Archaea is not enclosed in a nucleus, so they are called **prokaryotes**.

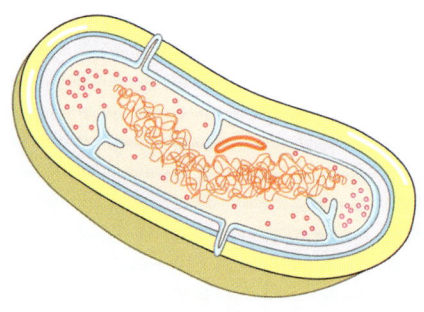
▲ The main difference between Bacteria and Archaea is in the biochemistry of their cells

Where in the World?

Bacteria and Archaea live everywhere except the coldest environments. They live in ponds and lakes, in the soil, in rotting food, in the ocean, and even inside you! The ones that live inside you are of two types. The first kind are called pathogens and they cause diseases. The other kind are **symbionts** that help you digest food, make vitamins, and keep pathogens out.

Extremophiles

Many species of Bacteria and Archaea can live in environments which are dangerous for other organisms. These are called extremophiles. Many of them have been studied by microbiologists as they can provide valuable drugs and chemicals for industrial uses.

◄ The Morning Glory hot spring in Yellowstone National Park. Its amazing colour comes from the thermophilic microbes growing in it

💡 Isn't It Amazing!

Bacteria can feed on anything. The species *Ideonella sakaensis* can live off polyethylene terephthalate, which is used for making plastic bottles.

▲ Scientists are looking for Bacteria and Archaea that can break down plastic into CO_2

Name	Grow in
Acidophiles	acidic soil or water of pH 1–5
Alkaliphiles	alkaline soil or water of pH above 9
Halophile	soil or water with high amounts of salt
Thermophiles	water whose temperature is between 60–80°C
Hyperthermophiles	at temperatures above 80°C
Psychrophiles	at temperatures of 15°C or lower (but will freeze below 0°C)
Piezophiles or Barophiles	at high hydrostatic pressure, like the bottom of the ocean
Oligotrophes	soil or water poor in nutrients
Endolithic microbes	rock or minerals
Xerophiles	soils that have very little water

Fungi

Fungi make up a kingdom by themselves and grow everywhere. Mushrooms, truffles, yeast, and moulds are all fungi. They grow mostly in the soil, but also in spoiled food, stagnant water, and other places.

How to Find Fungi

You can identify fungi easily by their net-like body, called **mycelium**. Sticking out from the mycelia are tiny pin-like bodies called **sporangia**. These contain spores, which are the 'seeds' of fungi. They travel in the air and settle in new places where the fungus can grow. Fungal spores can withstand heat, dryness and even pesticides. But you also need fungi, especially yeast, to make bread, wine and many kinds of cheese.

◀ *Bread turns mouldy because of the growth of Penicillium or Aspergillus fungi*

Classification of Fungi

Fungi are divided into seven phyla on the basis of DNA studies:

- **Chytridiomycota:** Aquatic fungi
- **Neocallimastigomycota:** Fungi found in the intestines of cows, horses and deer
- **Blastocladiomycota:** Parasitic fungi, especially on fruits
- **Microsporidia:** Unicellular fungi parasitic on other unicellular life forms
- **Glomeromycota:** Fungi that symbiotically live with plant roots (**mycorrhiza**)
- **Ascomycota:** Parasitic fungi of plants, including truffles, yeasts, and many antibiotic-making fungi
- **Basidiomycota:** Parasitic fungi of plants that cause rust. This phyla also comprises of **mushrooms**

▲ *Toadstools that grow in a circle are called fairy rings*

Incredible Individuals

Fungi live in places where they are regularly attacked by bacteria. They protect themselves by releasing chemicals into the environment, which prevent bacteria from growing. The first of these was discovered by Alexander Fleming. He saw that a fungus called Penicillium had killed the bacterial cultures he had preserved in petri dishes. He soon found the chemical that was doing this and named it **Penicillin**. Ever since then, scientists have discovered hundreds of such chemicals from fungi, which we call antibiotics.

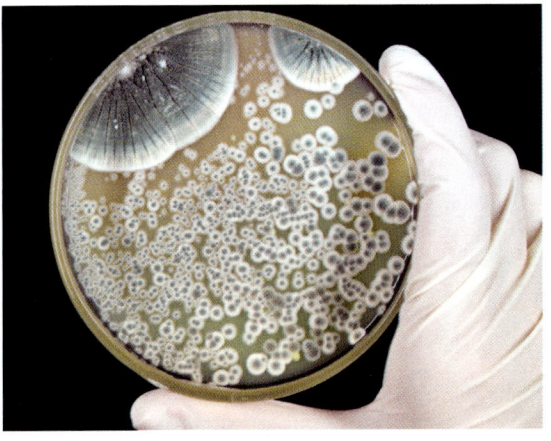

▲ *The species Penicillium roqueforti is used to make blue cheese*

Toadstools

Toadstool is a common word for mushrooms that are poisonous, but there's no way to tell which ones are poisonous unless you are an expert.

Inside a Plant

When you think of a plant, you usually think of something that has green leaves and brightly-coloured flowers. This is an angiosperm, the most successful group of plants. But did you know that plants also include algae, moss, ferns, grasses and herbs, alongside shrubs and trees?

Kingdom Plantae

Algae form a kingdom of their own, while the rest are members of kingdom Plantae. Many plant species were wiped out during **mass extinction**; so, many of the plants we see evolved just a few million years ago. A typical 'plant' has roots, stems, leaves, and flowers—but many of the simpler plants are not organised this way.

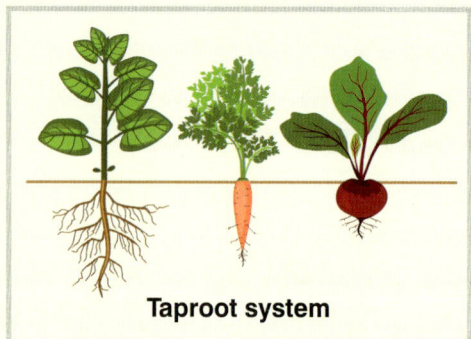
Taproot system

Fibrous root system

Root

The roots of a plant anchor it to the ground and pull in water and minerals from the soil. Different kinds of plants have different roots. Most monocots and 'lower plants' have **fibrous roots**, which emerge from the level of the ground and go underground in different directions. Most dicots have **taproots**, which have a main root that gives off branches. Many root vegetables are made of taproots that have been modified by evolution to store starch, so that the plant can 'winter over' to the next season, i.e. be able to survive underground in winter without **photosynthesis**.

◀ Onions and potatoes also grow underground, but they are modified stems, not roots

▶ Trees have three important organs; roots, leaves, and the stem—which may have branches

▲ Lawn grass with a well-developed fibrous root system

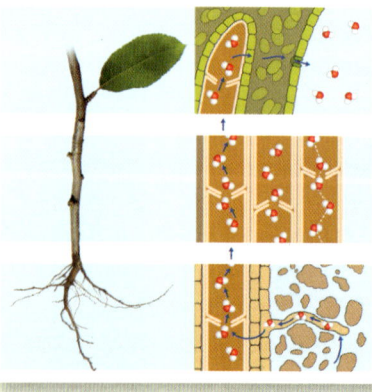
▲ Water travels by capillary action from the roots to the leaves, where it combines with CO_2 to form glucose by photosynthesis

Stem

The stem is the part of the plant that grows above the ground. In most plants, it is soft and green, but in trees it grows to become wide and woody as a thick bark made of lots of dead cells. The main job of the stem is to carry water from the roots to the leaves and flowers. It does so through two sets of tubes called the xylem and phloem. The xylem carries water upwards through capillary action, while the phloem carries minerals. Plant stems are divided into long intervals called internodes, separated by nodes. The nodes are the place from which the branches and leaves grow.

Leaf

Leaves are the most complex organs of a plant. The upper surface of a leaf is made of a waterproof cuticle and a protective layer called palisade mesophyll. The lower part has tiny openings called stomata (singular: stoma) through which the plant 'breathes in' carbon dioxide during daytime. The veins of the leaf bring water from the roots. Carbon dioxide reacts with water in the spongy mesophyll to make glucose by photosynthesis.

All plant cells contain a chemical called **chlorophyll**, which is required to make glucose. Chlorophyll traps energy from sunlight and passes it on to the leaf's enzymes for photosynthesis. It is chlorophyll that gives plants their green colour.

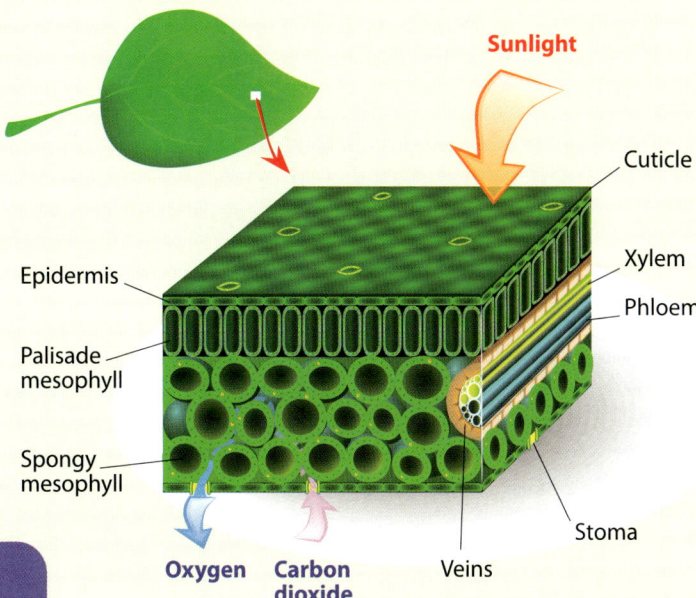

▲ At night, photosynthesis stops, and the plants use the food to grow, releasing CO_2 again. That is why it is said that you should not sit under trees at night

In Real Life

The world's tallest tree is a giant sequoia in the USA named General Sherman. Its xylem is therefore the world's longest natural column of water.

▶ General Sherman is 84 metres tall

Isn't It Amazing!

Did you know that lichens are made of two kingdoms cooperating with each other to make a living together? There are many different types of lichens, but each is made of a fungus and an alga (singular form of algae). This is called symbiosis.

▲ The lichen's alga makes food for the fungus, while the fungus takes in water and minerals for the alga

Algae, Bryophytes and Pteridophytes

Some plants evolved from single-celled organisms. They are known for their ability to make their own food by the process of photosynthesis. They reproduce in two ways—by making asexual spores in one generation, and male and female sexual gametes in the next generation. Although they have left behind very few fossils, we know that they might have evolved over 500 million years ago.

In Real Life

Sargasso is a kind of alga that grows while floating on seawater. There is so much of it in the Atlantic Ocean between Bermuda and Florida that the area is called the Sargasso Sea.

▲ The algae in the Sargasso Sea capture much of the plastic waste we release into the oceans

Algae

Algae make up many kingdoms of their own and are found in all parts of the world. They may be single-celled or made of many cells clumped together as filaments or sheets. Algal blooms form on ponds and lakes which may be polluted with sewage or faecal matter. The Red Sea gets its name from frequent blooms of red algae. They often appear as shiny sheets on the surface and are called pond scum.

Bryophytes

These include the liverworts, hornworts mosses, and other plants that often grow where no other plants grow. They have a simple body structure without stems or leaves or roots. Instead, they have tissue called rhizoids that go underground to absorb water and minerals.

▲ Bryophytes grow in difficult terrains like walls and rocks

Pteridophytes

Ferns, club mosses, spike mosses, quillworts, horsetails, and whisks make up the **pteridophytes**. They evolved over 400 years ago and dominated Earth before the evolution of the higher plants (the **gymnosperms** and angiosperms). They have two forms. Long-living, larger-sized sporophytes make **asexual spores**, which grow up to make smaller, short-lived **gametophytes**. These make male and female gametes that merge to give rise to a new sporophyte. This is called alternation of generations.

▲ The fossils of ancient ferns make up most of the coal reserves of the world

▼ Algae are a very diverse group of organisms. Many sea organisms depend on them for food

► Algae that grow in the sea are called kelp or seaweed and are used in making dishes such as sushi

Gymnosperms

The scientific word 'gymnosperm' means 'naked seed'. The seeds of a gymnosperm are not enclosed in a fruit. On the other hand, angiosperms have seeds which are enclosed in fruits.

Where Do They Grow?

Some gymnosperms (like pines and firs) grow in the temperate regions of the world, making up the great pine forests of Canada and Russia. Other gymnosperms, like cycads, grow in the tropics. Plants that shed all their leaves either in summer or winter are called deciduous. On the other hand, gymnosperms are called **evergreen** because new leaves grow as old ones fall off.

◀ *Evergreen trees like pines keep their leaves in winter too*

Pine Reproduction

▲ *Squirrels play an important role in dispersing pine seeds*

Pine seeds grow on a special branch called a cone. Therefore, pine trees are called conifers. Cones may be male (bearing pollen) or female (bearing eggs). The pollen is carried by wind to the eggs of other pine trees. Pollen and eggs join to become one cell called the **embryo**; this is called **fertilisation**. The embryo grows to become a pine seed over 2–3 years. Squirrels and other animals that eat the cones carry the seeds with them and drop them in a new place. Scientists call this **germination**.

▲ *Pine seeds are used in desserts and other dishes*

Isn't It Amazing!

Over 250 million years ago, plants of the order Ginkgoales were spread throughout the Earth but became extinct soon after. However, one species survived the apocalypse—Ginkgo biloba—and it still grows in temple gardens in China and Japan.

▲ *Ginkgo fossil compared to a fresh ginkgo leaf. Ginkgo is called a living fossil*

Pine Pollen and Ice Ages

Palynology is the study of pollen from soil. The deeper the soil, the older it is, because new soil is deposited on top as dust every year. Scientists use pollen to find out how Earth's climate was in the past, and what plants grew then. As pine trees grow in cold climates, if you see their pollen from soil samples in the tropics, it tells you that there was an ice age in the past.

Pine pollen under a microscope ▶

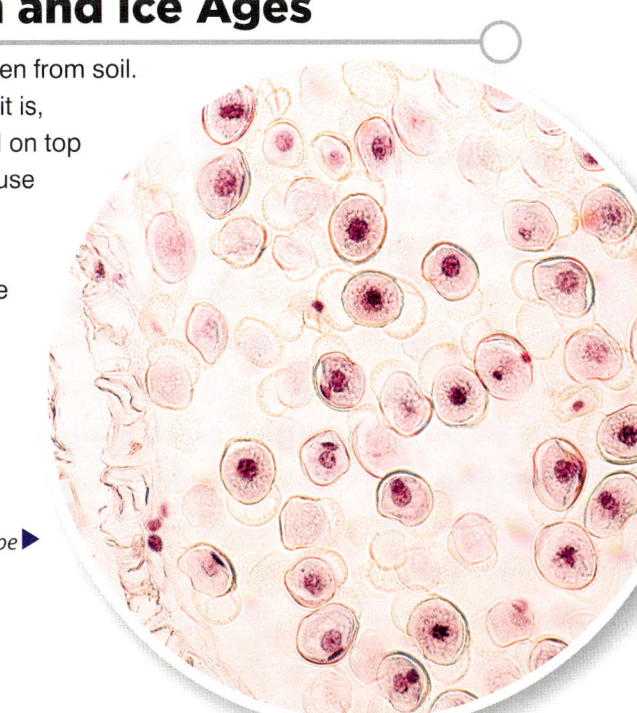

Angiosperms

When we think of plants, we really think of the angiosperms, which botanists call flowering plants. They make 80 per cent of all plants on our planet today. They can be divided into two types—dicots and monocots. Dicots include all the plants with pretty flowers like roses, dahlias, and chrysanthemums. They also include plants which give us most of our fruits and vegetables like mangoes, oranges, carrots, and tomatoes. Monocots include grasses and most of our crop plants like rice, wheat, corn, barley, oats, millets, and more.

▲ There are about 3,00,000 species of angiosperms worldwide, most in the tropics

Dicots vs Monocots

Take a dicot seed, like a bean, and you can split it into two. Each of these halves is called a cotyledon. Monocots only have one cotyledon. Monocots and dicots also have other differences.

Monocots	Dicots
They have 3 petals and sepals.	They have 4–5 petals and sepals.
Leaf veins are parallel.	Leaf veins are branched.
Xylem and phloem are scattered in the stem.	Xylem and phloem form a ring.
They have fibrous roots.	They have taproots.
They are rarely branched.	Most dicots are branched.

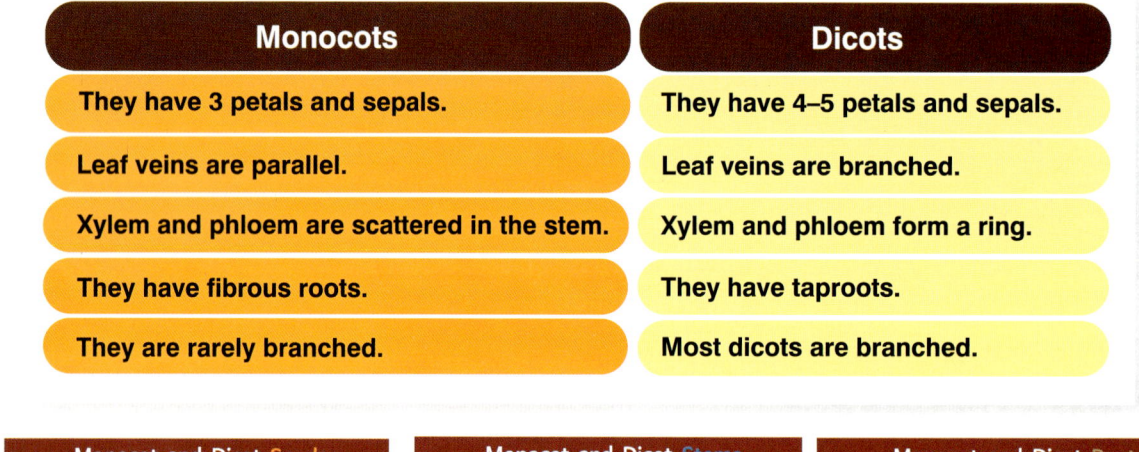

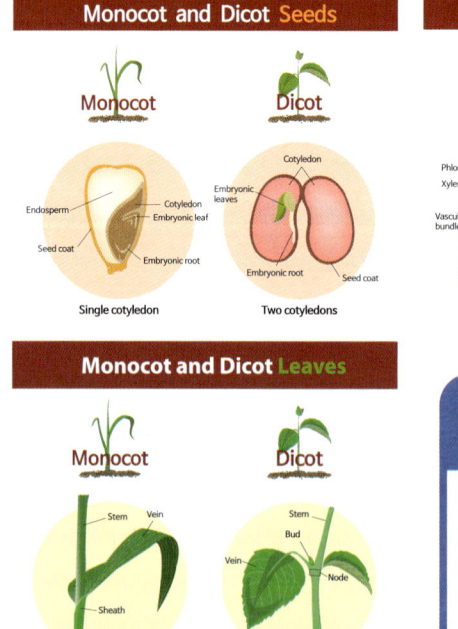

▲ Monocots and dicots provide us with almost everything we eat

In Real Life

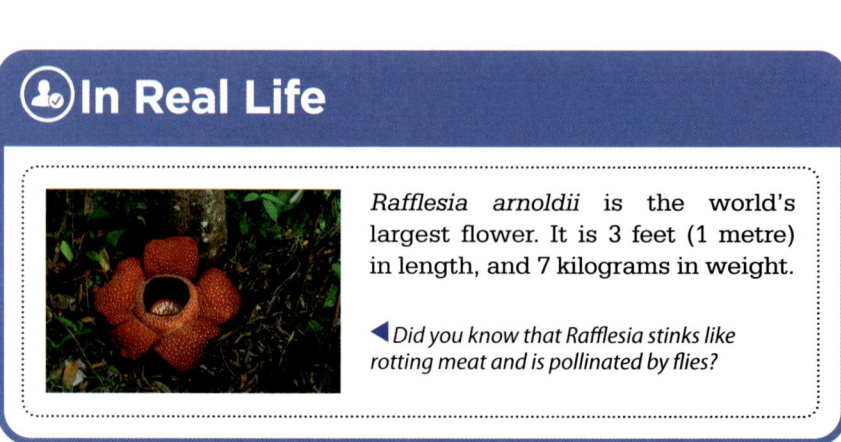

Rafflesia arnoldii is the world's largest flower. It is 3 feet (1 metre) in length, and 7 kilograms in weight.

◂ Did you know that Rafflesia stinks like rotting meat and is pollinated by flies?

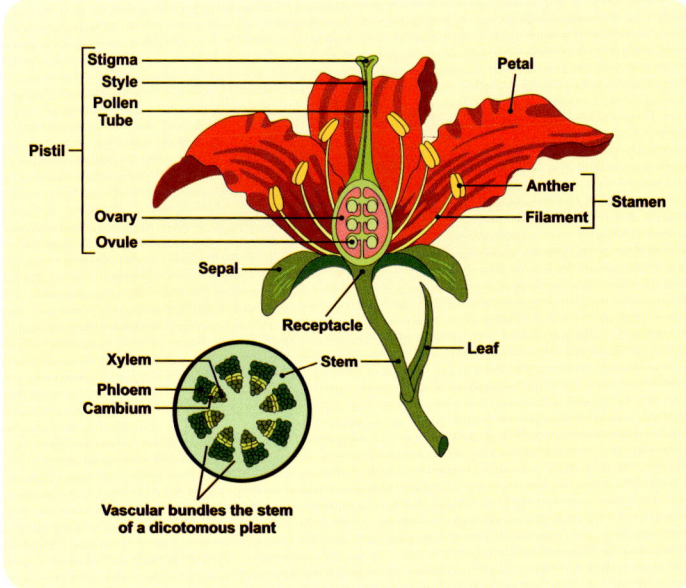

▲ Parts of a flower

Incredible Individuals

Carolus Linnaeus (1707–78) was a Swedish naturalist with an obsession for classifying things. He divided the whole living world into two kingdoms—plants and animals. Each kingdom was divided into classes, genera and species. Though many of his classifications have now been changed, his hierarchical system is still in use, as is his system of giving scientific names which remain the same in all languages.

◀ A sculpture of Linnaeus in the Chicago Botanical Garden

Flower

Did you know that a flower is not one organ, but four? The outermost parts—sepals (green) and petals (coloured)—help to protect the flower, and also attract insects and birds. The inner parts are the male organ androecium, which makes pollen, and the female organ gynoecium, which makes the egg. Pollination happens when pollen from one flower reaches the egg of another flower, often on a different plant.

Pollination

Different plants have different ways of getting their pollen to another flower. Some have bright flowers, and at the deep end of the flower is a small pool of sugary liquid called nectar. Insects like bees and butterflies like this nectar. When they come to drink it, the pollen sticks all over their bodies. When they go to another flower, the pollen is picked up by that flower. Other plants have small flowers, and their pollen is picked up by the wind.

◀ Yellow flowers attract honeybees and bumblebees, while red flowers attract small birds

Seed Dispersal

After pollination, the egg of the flower turns into a seed, while the remaining parts fall away. In some plants, the seed is enclosed in a fleshy fruit (like berries), while in some it is inside a papery pod (like peas), and in others, it is inside a wooden nut (like walnuts).

Plants that make fruits and nuts depend on animals that eat them and throw away the seed, which makes a new plant if it finds new ground. Plants that make pods wait till the pod dries, which then cracks open with a bang, flinging the seeds many metres or yards away.

▶ Dandelion seeds have feathery stems that help them float away in the wind till they can land on new ground

Inside an Invertebrate

Most biologists divide the animal kingdom into invertebrates and vertebrates. Although advances in taxonomy have shown that this is not a scientific way to classify animals, it is still useful for many reasons. Invertebrates are animals that do not have a hard skeleton, or have their bodies organised into complex organ systems. Vertebrates are abundantly seen in the fossil record of the planet because they leave behind bones that can become fossils. Invertebrates are made of soft tissue, which decays after death, leaving behind no trace of the animal.

▲ Invertebrate bodies are made of many segments. In many species, a single segment can regrow the rest of the animal

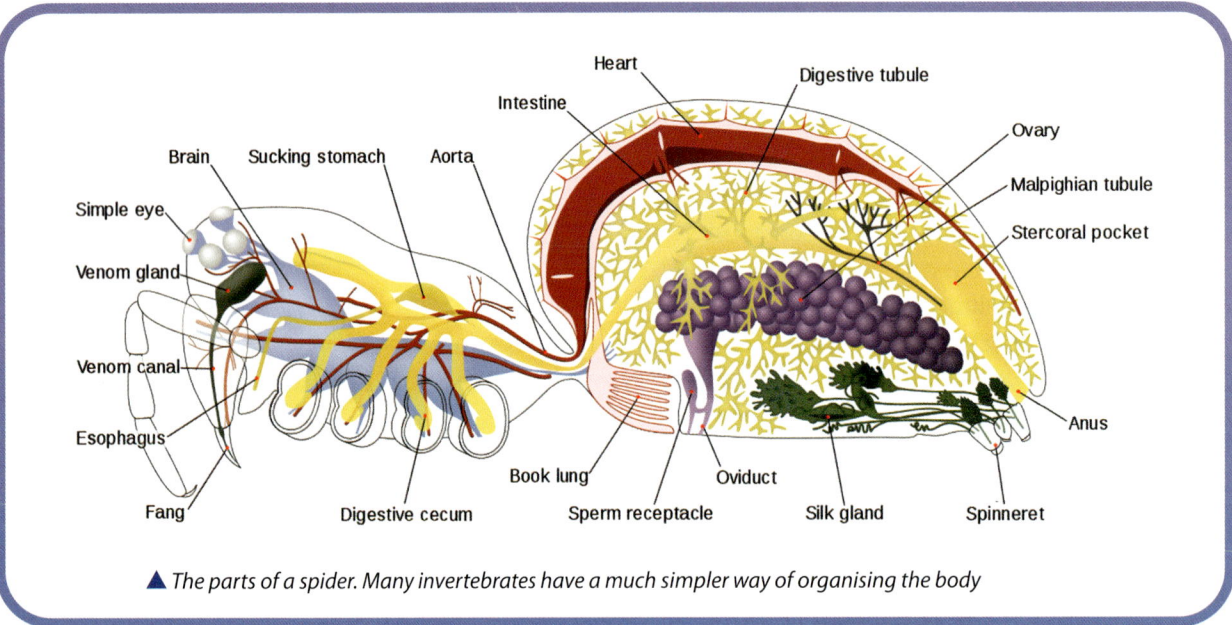

▲ The parts of a spider. Many invertebrates have a much simpler way of organising the body

🔍 Anatomy

Invertebrate anatomy differs very starkly from that of vertebrates. Here we will discuss the anatomy of Arthropods (insects, spiders, and crustaceans), which make up the largest and most diverse phylum of the animal kingdom.

Many invertebrates cannot swallow their food like we do. Instead, they squirt digestive enzymes onto the food (which may be rotting fruit, insects, or other animals), and suck in the digested juice. Invertebrates breathe in many ways. Animals like spiders have book lungs, while others have spiracles or gills. These take in air directly through the tissues.

Invertebrate blood is called haemolymph, and carries food absorbed from their intestines to the rest of the tissues. Most (except Arthropods and Molluscs) lack a brain and spinal cord; instead, a neural net made of ganglia controls their senses and movements. Many invertebrates have sophisticated sensory organs, such as compound eyes, antennae (for smell and touch), and taste buds on their feet.

◀ Spiders spit digestive enzymes onto their prey and suck in the remains

👤 In Real Life

The nervous system of the squid is made of nerve cells that have axons with wide diameters. These were used by Alan Hodgkin and Andrew Huxley to work out how the nerves conduct messages, for which they received the Nobel Prize in 1963.

▲ A squid's axon can be up to 1mm in diameter—50 times that of a crab, and 1,000 times that of a human

Classification

The classification of invertebrates is now based on DNA sequencing. However, earlier it was based on comparing various features such as body cavity, the number of appendages, the symmetry of the body etc. Today, biologists recognise 34 phyla of invertebrates.

The simplest are called Parazoa—those that are barely like animals, including sponges and placozoans. These are made of cells of the same type, not organised into tissues. Next come the Coelenterates, which include animals like jellyfish. These have very basic tissues. Following these are a number of phyla together called Helminths—including flatworms, roundworms, and rotifers.

Annelids are a phylum of worms made of segmented bodies, like earthworms. The adaptive benefit of these is that each segment can function entirely on its own, even if the animal is cut in two. Annelids gave rise to Arthropods, which are the most abundant phylum of animals today, and Molluscs, which include both shelled animals like snails and oysters, and shell-less animals like squids and octopi. After them come the Echinoderms which include starfish, sea urchins, and sea cucumbers.

▲ *Jellyfish are among the oldest animal species, having lived for over 500 million years*

◀ *Beetles are the most diverse group of invertebrates, with over 83,000 species*

Invertebrates
Animals without backbone

Worms	Arthropods	Cnidarians	Echinoderms	Mollusks	Sponges
They are animals with soft, tube-shaped bodies and a distinct head. Some worms live inside other animals, others live in the water or on land. They eat living organisms such as nematode, protozoan, rotifer, bacteria, fungi	They have legs and some have wings. They live on land, in the water and in the air. They eat fungi, worms, or other arthropods	They have a central opening surrounded by tentacles. They live in water. They take in food and eliminate waste through the central opening	Their bodies are covered in spikes or spines. They live in water. They have a central opening for taking in food	Soft-bodies with external or internal shells. Some live on land and others live in water. They have a muscular foot that allows them to move and hunt for food	They are the simplest invertebrates. They live in water. They filter food from the water that surrounds them

▲ *Scientifically, the kingdom Animalia is divided into 35 phyla, of which invertebrates make up 34*

▲ *Gastropods with shells are called snails, while those without shells are called slugs*

Isn't It Amazing!

Unlike vertebrates, the intestines of invertebrates, especially insects, have an acidic environment. The bacterium *Bacillus thuringiensis* makes a protein that turns into crystals in this environment. These crystals plug the intestine and the insect starves. This gene has been transferred by genetic engineers into plants like cotton to make them resistant to pests.

▶ *Bt Cotton, a genetically engineered form of cotton, resistant to insects*

Parazoa and Radiata

The phyla on this page represent the very beginning of the animal kingdom. Some are no more than a bunch of cells clumped together to feed and protect themselves. In other phyla, we see tissues beginning to emerge. In these animals, cells have different jobs, like some ingest food while others protect from predators, and so on. They reproduce asexually, which means they can simply split into two halves, each of which makes a new organism.

Porifera and Placozoa

The Porifera and Placozoa are two phyla which are together called Parazoa, which means 'nearly animals'. The Porifera (sponges) are little more than a sheet of cells rolled into a tube. Water passes into the opening of the tube (osculum), and filters through the body. The cells grab and eat up bacteria and other one-celled organisms as they pass. This is called filter-feeding. Only one genus makes up the phylum Placozoa and it is the *Trichoplax*, which looks like floating dandruff.

▲ Sponges emerged on Earth over 541 million years ago

▶ The scientific name of jellyfish is Medusa, since it resembles the Gorgon of Greek mythology

Coelenterates

These are animals that look like blobs floating in the water, but they have nerve cells and muscle cells. There is an outer sheet of cells called the ectoderm which protects the body, and an inner sheet called the endoderm which digests food. The nerve cells make up a network called the nerve net. Some cells are arranged into long tentacles, at the end of which are stinging cells which inject venom into their prey.

In Real Life

The Portugese Man o' War resembles a jellyfish, but it is a siphonophore. A colonial organism madea of small creature called zooids, that make up a gas-filled float that travels the waters. Despite its strong venom, the Bluebottle fish *(Nomeus gronovii)* lives among the tentacles. It takes care not to get stung, but has adapted to survive in its chosen home.

▼ Portuguese Man o' War

Helminths and Annelids

The Helminths and Annelids are phyla which have a range of lifestyles. They might live on the seabed or underground. They also show the evolution of organs, body cavities, and different methods of reproduction.

Acoelomates

Acoelomates are animals that do not have a body cavity, so they are called flatworms. They have no blood or gills, so they breathe through their skin. Some, like tapeworms, are parasitic, while others live on the sea floor.

▶ *The bright colours of this flatworm act as a warning to predators that it is poisonous*

Pseudocoelomates

Pseudocoelomates are a group of tiny animals that are found almost everywhere. They have nerves but not a nervous system, and a digestive system not attached to the body by muscles. They include Nematoda (roundworms) and Rotifera (wheeled animals).

◀ *Rotifers make up most of the zooplankton that whales and other filter-feeders eat*

Coelomates

Coelomates are those who have a true body cavity in which all their organs are present. The inner part of the cavity is made of the digestive system and the outer part by the skin. Earthworms, insects, fish, and human beings are all coelomates. The phyla Annelida (earthworms) and Arthropoda also have a segmented body plan.

◀ *Earthworms eat and excrete their whole bodyweight in a day*

💡 Isn't It Amazing!

As they eat, earthworms enrich the soil with phosphorus and nitrogen, help water reach deep within the soil, and help the soil particles stick better to each other. Many farmers introduce earthworms to make soil fertile. This is called vermicomposting.

▲ *The presence of earthworms in soil indicates that it is fertile*

Reproduction

If both males and females are required to make a baby, the animal (or plant) is called sexual. Some animals and plants can reproduce by breaking off a part of their body—they are called asexual. Earthworms are hermaphrodites, that is, both male and female organs are present in the same animal.

Protostome Coelomates

Protostome is a word that scientists use to describe animals whose first body opening during their development becomes their mouth. They consist of many phyla, many of which were common over 500 million years ago but are now rare. However, two of them make up the most common animals on land and sea—Arthropods and Molluscs.

▲ The phyla Tardigrada, Brachiopoda, and Bryozoa are made of tiny animals together called zooplankton

Arthropoda

Arthropods are the most abundant animals on land. The word 'arthropod' means 'jointed feet'. All the animals belonging to this group have jointed legs. They include:
- **Chelicerata:** Over 77,000 species including horseshoe crabs, spiders and sea-spiders
- **Crustacea:** Over 52,000 species including crabs, shrimp, prawns and krill
- **Myriapoda:** Over 13,000 species including centipedes and millipedes
- **Insecta:** Over 1 million species

Insecta are further divided into different groups of species.

Species	Examples
Zygentoma	Silverfish
Archaeognatha	Jumping bristletails
Ephemeroptera	Mayflies
Odonata	Dragonflies
Plecoptera	Stoneflies
Blattodea	Cockroaches
Notoptera	Gladiator bugs
Phasmatoptera	Stick insects
Orthoptera	Grasshoppers
Dermaptera	Earwigs
Phthiraptera	Lice
Thysanoptera	Thrips
Hemiptera	True bugs
Homoptera	Cicadas
Megaloptera	Alderflies
Neuroptera	Lacewings
Mecoptera	Scorpionflies
Trichoptera	Caddisflies
Lepidoptera	Butterflies
Coleoptera	Beetles
Hymenoptera	Ants, bees and wasps
Diptera	True flies
Siphonaptera	Fleas

▲ Phylum Arthropoda includes 84 per cent of animals that live on land

Incredible Individuals

Bees, ants, wasps, and termites are eusocial insects, that is, they are social insects amongst which some exist only to help their family, led by the queen. In bees, the workers have a unique dance language by which they tell other bees where to find nectar and pollen, which is what they eat. Karl von Frisch spent his lifetime trying to work out this fascinating language. He managed to translate for us the meaning of the waggle dance, where bees move and make the figure 8 to tell each other where the food is. He won the Nobel Prize for Physiology or Medicine for this research.

▶ A worker who has found food will 'dance' to tell others where to look for it and how much food there is

Molluscs

Barring land snails, all animals of this phylum live in the sea. They are divided into shelled and shell-less animals. Those without shells come under the classes Aplacophora, Polyplacophora and Monoplacophora. Clams, mussels, oysters, scallops, shipworms, and cockles all make up class Bivalvia, which have two shells each. Limpets, snails, and slugs make up class Gastropoda, which have coiled shells. But the most notable is class Cephalopoda (nautiluses, cuttlefishes, squids and octopuses), famous for their long tentacles, ink glands, and movement by shooting jets of water.

▲ Squid and cuttlefish grow to be among the largest invertebrates in the world

Deuterostome Coelomates

Deuterostome is a word that scientists use to describe animals whose first body opening during development becomes their anus (the second one becomes the mouth). These were rare over 500 million years ago, but are now common, including Chaetognatha (arrow worms), Echinodermata (starfish), Hemichordata (acorn worms), and Chordata (fish, amphibians, reptiles, birds, and mammals).

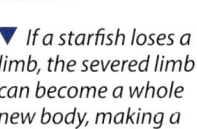
◀ The acorn worm, representative of the Hemichordates

Echinoderms

This phylum with 7,000 species includes starfish, brittle stars, sea urchins and sea cucumbers. Animals of this phylum do not move about much. Unlike other animals which have a left side and a right side (bilateral symmetry), they have radial symmetry, so they can have up to five sides. They are covered with a thick exoskeleton, so many fossils of this phylum have survived from ancient times.

▼ If a starfish loses a limb, the severed limb can become a whole new body, making a new starfish

▲ Echinoderms are named for their spiny (echino) skins (derma), from the Greek language

Protochordates

These animals are a bridge between invertebrates and the animals that finally evolved into vertebrates. They include the Hemichordata—which are worm-like animals that breathe through gills, and the Urochordata—which have a notochord, a rod-like organ made of cartilage that forms a simple endoskeleton. But as they grow up, the animals lose their heads and notochord and develop a tunic around their body, through which they filter plankton to eat.

▲ Tunicates show reverse development in the animal kingdom

Cephalochordates

The Cephalochordata are members of phylum Chordata, but they do not have a backbone that encloses the spinal cord, so they are still considered to be invertebrates. Instead of a backbone, they have a notochord and muscles attached to them, but no circulatory system or heart.

Giving Birth

Except for mammals, all animals are oviparous, which means that they lay eggs to reproduce. Their eggs may be naked or covered with a thick shell made of calcium carbonate. The baby grows within the egg, and when it is ready to come out, the egg breaks. The baby is ready to come out when all its organs have fully developed. On the other hand, mammals are viviparous. It means that the baby develops inside its mother, who gives birth when she and the baby are fully ready. Some animals keep the eggs within the body until they hatch, like seahorses. These are called ovoviviparous.

Inside a Vertebrate

Vertebrates are what we think of when we say 'animal'. Elephants, ostriches, crocodiles, frogs, salmon, and sharks are all vertebrates. They deserve the title, for although they come late in the fossil record (just a few hundred million years ago), today they have become the most dominant animal life forms on the planet. They live almost everywhere, from the bottom of the oceans to the tops of mountains, from the ice sheets of Greenland to the raging desert of the Sahara. Yet, in spite of their diversity, their bodies are remarkably similar on the inside.

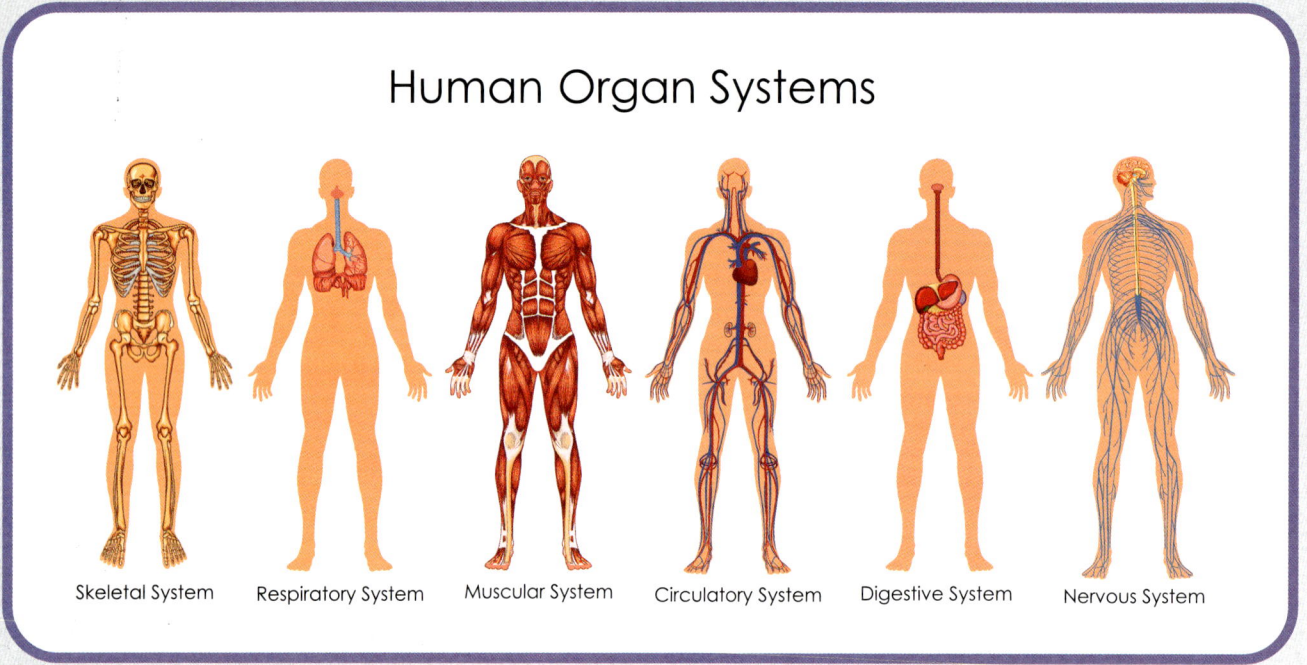

▲ The name 'vertebrate' comes from the bones of the backbone (vertebra) that are common to all in this phylum

🔍 Anatomy

All vertebrates are made of organ systems, in which different organs link up to form a functional part of the animal. Many organ systems have continued from our invertebrate ancestors but have become more complex. The digestive system and the nervous system are examples of this. The digestive system has many glands and has an alkaline environment, while the nervous system has a large brain and a prominent spinal cord.

Others have evolved anew, like the respiratory system and the skeletal system. Invertebrates depend on an exoskeleton to give them shape, while vertebrates are made of a new type of organ called the bone, to which the muscles attach. The respiratory system does not carry air directly to the tissues but depends on a new molecule called haemoglobin, which evolved with the vertebrates.

The circulatory system and the muscular system are a mix of old and new organ systems. The circulatory system does not just transport food, but also carries oxygen to the tissues from the gills or lungs. The muscular system is also more sophisticated, with the emergence of voluntary and involuntary muscles.

▲ An elephant's spine is very unique. Instead of smooth, round spinal disks, they have sharp bony protrusions that extend upwards from their spine

◄ Fishes, amphibians, reptiles, birds and mammals are all vertebrates

SCIENCE | LIVING THINGS | 25

Heart

What makes vertebrates so successful? Some biologists say it is the evolution of the circulatory system that could now carry oxygen to the tissues, and a heart that keeps beating throughout life. As a regular supply of oxygen feeds the tissues, the animals get more energy to catch more food, and make more babies.

▲ Crocodiles are the only reptiles with four-chambered hearts

▶ A sea turtle has a backbone which is connected to its shell so the shell can never come off

Classification

Vertebrates are classified into two large groups. One group includes cold-blooded animals or poikilotherms, which cannot control their body temperature. The other group includes warm-blooded animals or homoiotherms, which can control their body temperature. The former group includes fish, amphibians, and reptiles, while the latter includes birds and mammals. Ever since they evolved, fish have dominated the seas, and the Age of the Fish is still ongoing there.

On land, the reptiles were the most dominant beings, culminating in the Age of Dinosaurs. Sadly, when a comet crashed into Earth 65 million years ago, it raised a dust cloud all over Earth so thick that it blocked the Sun and thousands of species became extinct, including many plants and dinosaurs. A new kind of animal became dominant on land and its age still continues. It is the Age of Mammals.

⭐ Incredible Individuals

Galen was a Roman doctor who studied the anatomy of animals by dissecting them. As dissecting human beings was not allowed by the Roman government, he dissected barbary apes instead, believing that their anatomy was very similar to ours.

▲ Galen, along with Hippocrates and Avicenna, is one of the three fathers of modern medicine

▲ Did you know that birds descended from dinosaurs?

▼ Vertebrates are the most successful phyla of animals after Arthropods

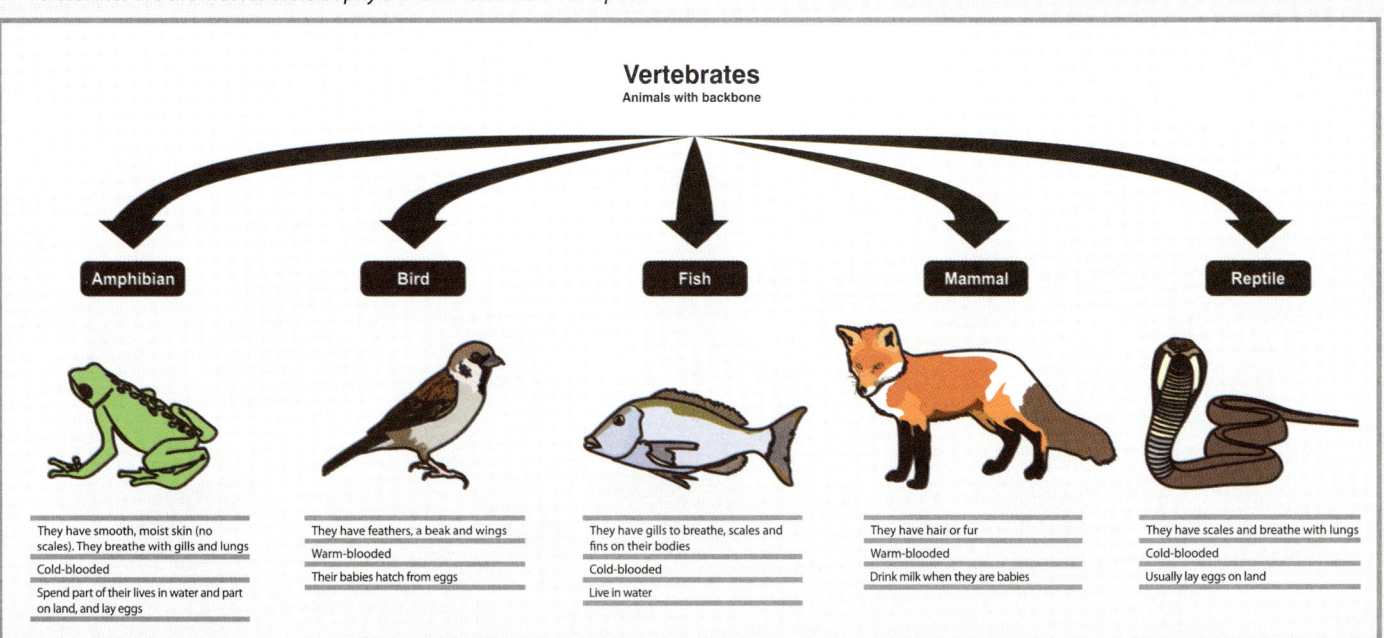

Vertebrates — Animals with backbone

Amphibian	Bird	Fish	Mammal	Reptile
They have smooth, moist skin (no scales). They breathe with gills and lungs	They have feathers, a beak and wings	They have gills to breathe, scales and fins on their bodies	They have hair or fur	They have scales and breathe with lungs
Cold-blooded	Warm-blooded	Cold-blooded	Warm-blooded	Cold-blooded
Spend part of their lives in water and part on land, and lay eggs	Their babies hatch from eggs	Live in water	Drink milk when they are babies	Usually lay eggs on land

Poikilotherms

Poikilotherm is a word used by scientists to describe animals who cannot control their body temperature. Though they are also called cold-blooded animals, their body temperature depends on the environment they are in. Because of this, most poikilotherms live in the tropics and warmer climates. Others that live in colder climates have various adaptations. For example, fish in Antarctic waters have special proteins that stop their blood from freezing. Others adapt by going into **hibernation**, during which they burrow themselves deep underground to save body heat, as the temperatures come close to freezing.

Jawless Fish (Agnatha)

This group includes lampreys and hagfishes. These animals do not have jaws, but a circular mouth instead.

Cartilaginous Fish (Chondrichthyes)

This class has 940 species including sharks, skates, stingrays, and sawfishes. Their skeletons are made entirely of cartilage, not bone.

▶ *Did you know that sharks' teeth never stop growing throughout their lives?*

Bony Fish (Osteichthyes)

These make up 33,000 of the 34,000 known species of fish. They include everything from salmon and seahorses, to eels and goldfish. Fish do not lay fertilised eggs like all other chordates. Instead, the female lays unfertilised eggs in a secure place (like under a rock), and the male 'spawns' over them. In seahorses, the female lays eggs in a special pouch that the male has, and the eggs develop in it till they hatch.

▲ *Many fish live in coral reefs, which gives them safe places to lay eggs and spawn*

Amphibians

The word 'amphibian' is of Greek origin and means 'double life'. That is true of class Amphibia, for they are almost different creatures on land and in water. The living orders of class Amphibia are Gymnophiona (snake-like caecilians, of which 170 species are known), Anura (frogs and toads, with over 5,400 species recorded) and Caudata (salamanders and newts, with over 550 species). They live mostly in the tropics and in various other habitats including rainforest trees, deserts, ponds, and rivers. They can breathe underwater through their skin, and on land through lungs.

▲ *Sadly, many amphibians are going extinct because their habitats are being destroyed for agriculture and industry*

SCIENCE | LIVING THINGS | 27

Reptiles

Class Reptilia is made of four living orders: order Testudinidae (tortoises, terrapins and turtles), order Crocodilia (crocodiles, alligators and caimans), order Sphenodontidae (tuataras), and order Squamata (lizards and snakes). It also has many extinct orders which make some of the world's most famous fossils—the dinosaurs, which include true dinosaurs, ichthyosaurs, archosaurs, pterodactyls, plesiosaurs, and mesosaurs.

Crocodiles have four-chambered hearts, which separate deoxygenated blood from oxygenated blood, while the rest have only three-chambered hearts. This makes them less sluggish than the rest.

▲ Reptiles range in size from 14mm (Nano-chameleon) to 8m (Saltwater Crocodile)

Dinosaurs

Dinosaurs can be divided into two main groups according to the shape of their hips: Saurischia (lizard-hips) and Ornithischia (bird-hips). Ornithischia includes Cerapoda (such as the genus *Triceratops*) and Thyreophora (such as the genus *Stegosaurus*). Saurischia were made of Sauropodomorpha, which includes the genus *Brontosaurus*, and Theropoda, which includes the famous *Tyrannosaurus rex* and the only surviving dinosaurs—birds.

⭐ Incredible Individuals

Mary Anning (1799–1847) discovered many of the world's famous fossils near the seaside town of Lyme Regis. She discovered ichthyosaurs, plesiosaurs, pterodactyls, and many others. But she got no credit for her discoveries, which instead went to male scientists.

▼ The tongue-twister 'She sells seashells on the seashore' was written in honour of Mary Anning

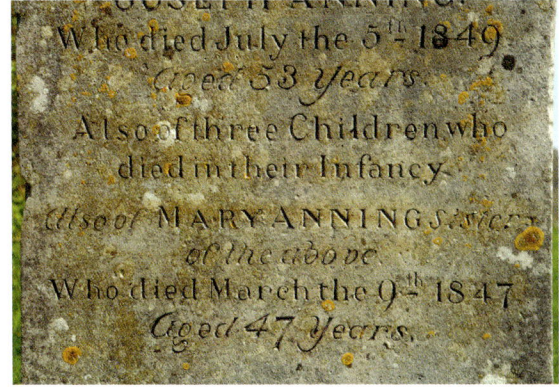

▲ People once thought that dinosaurs were sluggish and cold-blooded

💡 Isn't It Amazing!

Some scientists think that *Argentinosaurus* may have been the world's largest dinosaur, though no complete skeletons have been found. If confirmed, it would be the world's largest terrestrial animal, weighing 100 tonnes.

▲ *Argentinosaurus* is still half as big as the world's largest animal ever—the blue whale

Homoiotherms

The vertebrates who can control their body temperature are divided into two large classes. These are the birds (or aves) and the mammals. Mammals are in turn of three kinds—the egg-layers, the pouch-holders, and the true mammals. The common feature of all mammals is the mammary gland, which produces milk for their children. All other animals must find their own food from the day they are born, although in many species their parents will bring it to them for the first few months.

◀ *Modern research says that all birds evolved from a group of dinosaurs called the theropods*

Order	Examples
Passeriformes	Songbirds
Apodiformes	Hummingbirds
Piciformes	Woodpeckers
Charadriiformes	Gulls
Pteroclidiformes	Sandgrouse
Psittaciformes	Parrots
Columbiformes	Doves
Falconiformes	Raptors
Galliformes	Fowl
Gruiformes	Cranes
Procellariiformes	Albatrosses
Coraciiformes	Kingfishers
Strigiformes	Owls
Musophagiformes	Turacos
Cuculiformes	Cuckoos
Anseriformes	Waterfowl
Ciconiiformes	Storks
Caprimulgiformes	Nightjars
Pelecaniformes	Pelicans
Tinamiformes	Tinamous
Trogoniformes	Trogons
Podicipediformes	Grebes
Sphenisciformes	Penguins
Gaviiformes	Loons
Coliiformes	Mousebirds
Struthioniformes	Ostriches

Birds

Birds of a feather flock together, goes the old saying. For birds, this is quite literally true, as feathers (and beaks) are the common feature of all birds. Feathers help birds stay warm, not get wet, and, of course, to fly. Flightless birds like ostriches, emus, and kiwis make up the Palaeognathae, while the rest make up the Neognathae. There are over 9,000 species in 26 orders, of which songbirds (order Passeriformes) make 59 per cent of all birds.

Mammals

The 5,000 species of class Mammalia can be broadly divided into three types. Monotremes are the only mammals that lay eggs, and are found only in Australia. **Marsupials** include kangaroos, wallabies, koalas, and opossums. These mammals are found in Australia and South America. The placental or true mammals make up the rest, from the tiniest rodents and bats, to the largest elephants and whales. The females of

▲ *Marsupials give birth to live babies but carry them in a pouch (the marsupium) outside their bodies*

these species carry their babies inside their bodies in an amniotic sac. The baby is fed from the placenta and the umbilical cord, through which food, vitamins, minerals, and antibodies from the mother's blood enters the baby's blood. When the baby is finally ready to come into the world, the placenta breaks. The umbilical cord soon falls off, leaving a small mark called the navel or belly button. Rodents make up 42 per cent of all mammals, followed by bats, who make up 20 per cent.

▲ *Platypus were discovered in the 18th century by European explorers, but experts in Europe thought these were frauds, made of the body parts of various animals.*

Order	Examples
Tachyglossa	Echidnas
Platypoda	Platypus
Diprotodontia	Kangaroos
Dasyuromorphia	Carnivorous marsupials
Peramelemorphia	Bilbies
Notoryctemorphia	Marsupial moles
Microbiotheria	Monito del monte
Didelphimorphia	Opossums
Paucituberculata	Shrew-opossums
Rodentia	Rodents
Chiroptera	Bats
Soricomorpha	Shrews
Afrosoricida	Tenrecs
Erinaceomorpha	Hedgehogs
Primates	Monkeys
Artiodactyla	Cattle
Cetacea	Whales
Perissodactyla	Rhinos
Hyracoidea	Hyraxes
Sirenia	Manatees
Proboscidea	Elephants
Tubulidentata	Aardvark
Carnivora	Cats
Lagomorpha	Rabbits
Cingulata	Armadillos
Pilosa	Anteaters
Scandentia	Tree-shrews
Macroscelidea	Elephant-shrews
Pholidota	Pangolins

In Real Life

You know that the blue whale is the world's largest mammal, but which is the smallest? It is the bumblebee bat of Thailand, which grows to only 33 mm.

▼ *Did you know that female blue whales are larger than males?*

Incredible Individuals

The famous biologists Jane Goodall, Dianne Fossey, and Biruté Galdikas were picked by Louis Leakey to study chimpanzees, gorillas, and orangutans to better understand how human beings evolved.

▶ *Jane Goodall has been working with chimpanzees for over 60 years, and her discovery that they make and use tools was groundbreaking*

▲ *Orangutans, gorillas, chimpanzees, and human beings are together called the great apes*

Habitats

Habitat is the scientific word for the immediate environment in which a living organism can survive and reproduce. It includes the climate, food, terrain, predators, and the social group of males and females of its own species. Every organism is said to be adapted to its habitat, otherwise it will be driven extinct by other organisms that are better adapted. Look at this table and guess which animal we are talking about:

Habitat	Adaptation
Flat terrain with trees here and there	Walking on two flat feet with hands that can grip
A diet of fruits, roots, eggs and small animals	Teeth with small canines and square molars
A tropical climate that does not get too cold	Skin with hair but not fur, rich in melanin
Tool use and climbing	Opposable thumbs with power grip
Hunting	Binocular, colour vision
Throwing	Strong biceps and triceps
Complex social organisation	Large brain

All of this points to a primate whose natural habitat is the savanna of East Africa—human beings! Indeed, without cultural adaptations like making tools and wearing clothes, human beings cannot live in any other habitat naturally.

◀ *Olduvai Gorge, Tanzania, where our species is believed to have evolved*

🔍 Ecological Niche

The habitat to which each organism is fully adapted is called its ecological niche. Human beings have adapted themselves to a number of ecological niches, so they can live in Tibet, the Netherlands, Patagonia, Tanzania, and more. But most plants and animals can only live in one niche. For example, butterflies can only live in places where the weather is not too cold and lots of angiosperms grow because they live off the nectar of flowers; while the albatross makes the open sky its niche, where it can fly for days together.

▶ *King cobras occupy a niche in which they can eat other snakes*

👤 In Real Life

Many people have reported seeing an ancient animal (like a dinosaur, a water snake, or a dragon) in the Loch Ness in Scotland. But we know from studies of the habitat that nothing so large could live and breed there.

◀ *Loch Ness is too small to have enough food and resting space for a creature like the supposed Loch Ness Monster*

Island Biogeography

The theory of island biogeography says that if a species of a small animal got isolated on an island, it could grow to a bigger size since it escapes its predators. On the other hand, a species of a big animal will get smaller because it does not get enough to eat.

Isn't It Amazing!

Not many people thought that the theory of island biogeography applied to human beings until the discovery of the bones of an extinct species of humans on the island of Flores, Indonesia in 2003.

▲ Under 4 feet high, Homo floresiensis remains were nicknamed hobbits

Parasitism and Commensalism

Parasitism is a niche in which one organism lives off another (the host) without the other benefitting at all. Many disease-causing bacteria, fungi, leeches, lampreys, and even plants are parasitic. Commensals are similar to parasites but do not cause harm to their hosts.

▲ Banyan trees start out as parasites of other trees, before growing their own roots

Symbiosis

Symbiosis is a niche in which two organisms grow together and benefit each other. Lichens are an example of this. Another example is the bacteria in your large intestine. They give you vitamins, and you keep them safe.

Extinction

Biological extinction happens when too few members of a species are left for them to make enough babies for a sustainable population. Physical extinction occurs when the last individual of the species dies.

▶ The dodo, native to Mauritius, went extinct after the Dutch landed on the island and killed most of the birds

▼ Some ants live symbiotically with aphids. They keep them safe in exchange for a sugary drink the aphids make

Word Check

Abyssopelagic zone: The layer of the ocean 4,000 metres and below up to the ocean floor

Antibiotics: The chemicals made by fungi to protect themselves from bacteria

Asexual spore: A reproductive cell made by fungi and some plants without sexual reproduction

Bathypelagic zone: The layer of the ocean that starts from 1,000 metres from the surface and extends to 4,000 metres below the surface.

Cell membrane: It is the outer covering of a cell.

Cell wall: It is an extra covering outside the cell membrane.

Chlorophyll: It is a chemical that is present in all green plants that makes photosynthesis possible

Climatic zones: It is a region of the Earth, including the land and the ocean, where the climate is the same

Cytoplasm: It is the jelly that makes up most of the cell. It has water, proteins, fats and organelles in it.

Embryo: The youngest stage in the life of a multicellular organism

Endemic: Any living organism that grows in only one place and nowhere else.

Epipelagic zone: The layer of the ocean that starts from the surface and extends to 200 metres.

Evergreen: Plants which never shed all their leaves at the same time

Evolution: The process by which one species transforms into another, often over thousands of years.

Fertilisation: The process by which two sexual gametes unite to form an embryo

Fibrous roots: They are threadlike roots that grow from the base of the stem.

Gametophyte: It is the generation of a pteridophyte that makes sexual gametes

Genetic code: The set of rules by which information encoded in genetic material (DNA or RNA sequences) is translated into proteins (amino acid sequences) by living cells

Germination: The process by which a seed or spore gives rise to a fungus or plant

Gymnosperm: It is a plant that makes naked seeds

Habitable zone: It is the distance from a star where a planet can sustain life

Habitat: It is the natural home or environment of any living organism

Hibernation: The period in winter during which some animals sleep to preserve body heat

Living fossil: An organism which was abundant in a previous era but is now reduced to a small number of individuals

Marine beings: Any living thing that lives in the sea

Marsupials: Animals that carry their babies in a pouch on their body

Mass extinction: These were periods when many different life species suddenly went extinct.

Mesopelagic zone: The layer of the ocean that starts from 200 metres from the surface and reaches up to 100 metres from the surface.

Multicellular organism: A living thing made of more than one cell

Mycelium: The main body of a fungus from which root-like rhizomes and fruiting bodies (sporangia) branch off.

Mycorrhiza: It is a symbiotic association between a fungus and the roots of a vascular host plant.

Natural selection: The process by which a living thing adapted to its conditions survives and reproduces, while others that cannot adapt go extinct

Organism: It is the scientific name for any living thing

Pelagic: It is any biome that is present in the ocean

Photosynthesis: It is the process by which green plants make food from carbon dioxide and water in the presence of sunlight

Prokaryote: It is any living thing whose cells do not have a nucleus

Pteridophytes: It is a group of plants that has a vascular structure but produces no flowers or seeds.

Rainforests: They are dense forests in tropical areas which receive regular and heavy rainfall

Savanna: It is a biome in the tropical climatic zone which has strong winds and warm temperatures, where grain can be cultivated.

Sporangia: The part of a fungus and some other living things where spores are made

Symbiont: A living thing that lives closely with another species and protects it or makes food for it

Taiga: A climatic zone which has very cold temperatures, marked by forests of coniferous trees

Taproot: A primary root that grows vertically downward and gives off small lateral roots

Taxon (plural: taxa): A group of any rank, such as a species, family or class, in the classification according to taxonomy

Tidally locked: When a moon's rotation and revolution have the same period, it is said to be tidally locked to its planet

Tundra: A climatic zone which has such cold temperatures that it is covered by huge icesheets

Zoologist: A person who studies animals